Elihu, Innkeeper's Lad

Elihu, Innkeeper's Lad

Story by Dwyn Mounger
Illustrations by Gloria P. Weisz

Crippled Beagle Publishing
Knoxville, Tennessee

This work is protected by the copyright laws of the United States of America.
Copyright ©2018 by Dwyn Mounger. All rights reserved.

No part of this book may be reproduced or stored,
in whole or in part, in print or digital format,
without express permission by the author.

For information regarding permission, write to the publisher or author:
Crippled Beagle Publishing
5413 Glen Cove Drive, Knoxville, Tennessee 37919
dyer.cbpublishing@gmail.com

Dwyn Mounger
(865) 249-7731 ~ (904) 315-9312)
dwynmounger@gmail.com

Story by Dwyn Mounger
Illustrations by Gloria P. Weisz
Book Design by Jody Dyer

ISBN-13: 978-1-7321555-8-9

To our respective grandchildren Aiden, Annie, David, Ella, Jacob, Lillian, Mills, Owen, Peyton, and Timmons. May each of you, like Elihu, kneel at the manger!

I'm Elihu, innkeeper's lad,
and Bethlehem's my town.

I help my father with the guests
who stop here to bed down.

Our inn is simple--different from your hotels,
bright and clean.
We have no plumbing, rugs, or chairs—what's more,
no bed is seen!

Most guests bring with them little mats
and spread them on the floor,

Which really is no floor at all,
but hard-packed earth— no more.

But we've a roof and five small rooms
where travelers can sleep.

And in our courtyard stands a well with water,
cool and deep.

So seldom do our guests complain,
not even when we're packed
and have to crowd them in the rooms
with mats and blankets stacked.

Except—I never shall forget!
It happened one strange year.
So many travelers thronged our town!
They came from far and near.

They filled our rooms and courtyard, too.
They fought for space to sleep.

They pushed and shoved around our well.
They lay three, four, five deep!

My frantic father cried, "Quiet, please!
There's room for all in here!"

Our guests just laughed,
and some of them were drunk on wine, I fear.

My father sighed and shook his head.
He said, "Well, Elihu, Let's go back
to our family's room.
There's nothing we can do!"

I asked then, "Dad, who are these folks?
Why have they come to town?
What makes them crowd into our inn,
and fight so to bed down?"

He answered, "Son, you haven't heard?
The emperor in Rome
commands each family to go
to their ancestral home,
and there to register and learn
what taxes they must pay.
That's why old Bethlehem is packed
with travelers today."

I thought it strange, but asked no more,
for it was getting late.
I yawned, rolled out my mattress,
and lay down for sleep to wait.

But still our guests kept up their noise,
so loud we couldn't think.
The drunk folks sang,
and called to Dad, "Hey, bring us more to drink!"

My mother frowned and said to Dad,
"Oh, this will never do!
We grown-ups don't need sleep so much,
but what of Elihu?"

"I know!" I told my Mom and Dad.
I rose up with a leap.
"I'll go out to our backyard cave,
and with our cattle sleep!"

"I'm not afraid. The hay is warm.
Our good cow Ruth stays there.
The animals won't mind at all,
if I their bed now share."

"All right then, go," my mother said,
"but take this blanket, too.
And stay away from those drunk folks.
Be careful, Elihu!"

I took the blanket and a lamp,
walked through the outside door.
Above me in the sky I spied a million stars, or more.

I started for our barnyard cave,
but heard a sudden knock.
I looked around the corner,
toward the door we always lock.

A young man stood there in the dark.
He knocked and knocked again.
And on him leaned a tired young lass,
who seemed to sigh in pain.

Within our inn, the noisy guests
still laughed and drank and swore.
No one could hear the young man's knocks
and poundings on the door.

And so he shouted, "Open up!
We need a place to stay!
This woman's pregnant.
For God's sake, please don't turn us away!"

At last my father heard his cries,
pulled wide the heavy door.
"I'm sorry, but our inn is full," he said.
"We can't take more."

"And even if we could, you wouldn't want your wife
to sleep amid this noisy mob."
At this, the lass began to weep.

"She's soon to have a baby!"
cried the man in desperate plea.
"And we have walked from Nazareth,
up north, in Galilee!"

"I'm truly sorry," said my Dad.
"There's nothing I can do."
Just then an idea crossed my mind.
I cried, "Sir, I'll help you!"

The startled man looked up and asked,
"My boy, just who are you?"
I answered, "I'm the keeper's son.
My name is Elihu."

"I'm Joseph; this is Mary.
But please tell me what you mean.
How can you help us—
strangers, whom you've only just now seen?"

"I know a place," I answered,
"Where you both can safely rest.
Oh, Dad, I'll take them to our cave!
It's warm; the hay's the best!"

"Good idea, son! And, Joseph,
you and Mary stay for free.
I hope you don't mind animals.
The cave's our barn, you see."

"Oh no, I love them," Joseph said,
and thanked my Dad and me.
"Please take us there,
for Mary's now as tired as she can be."

"Just follow me; we'll soon be there,"
I said, my lamp held high.
"Now come inside. There's our cow Ruth.
Her manger stands nearby.

Don't mind the goats and sheep. They're friends.
The cat and dog are, too.
I'll fetch you water from the well.
Can I do else for you?"

"O, Elihu, how can we thank
a boy as kind as you?" said Mary.
"All we need is rest. This warm, clean cave will do."

I brought them water, then sank down
on my own mat and slept.
And they slept too.
In Bethl'hem's sky the stars their vigil kept.

Toward dawn, I woke up with a start.
I heard a Baby's cry!

Nearby stood Joseph wide awake.
He held a lamp up high.

Beside the manger of our cow,
kind Mary knelt and spread
her arms around a baby boy.
The manger was his bed.

So I knelt too, and Ruth the cow
mooed softly with delight.
Just then three shepherds stepped inside
and marveled at the sight.

"Why, here's the Babe Messiah King!" they cried.
"Tonight we heard the angel of the Lord himself
announce this wondrous word:
That here in Bethlehem was born
the Savior of the race.
And now, we shepherds worship him,
and see him face to face!"

"Come, Elihu, innkeeper's lad,"
good Mary cried with joy.

"Come, shepherds, too, I do not mind
—and touch this Jesus boy!"

There, lying in Ruth's manger,
then wee Jesus grasped my thumb.

I praised the Lord,
for now I knew the Christ had surely come!

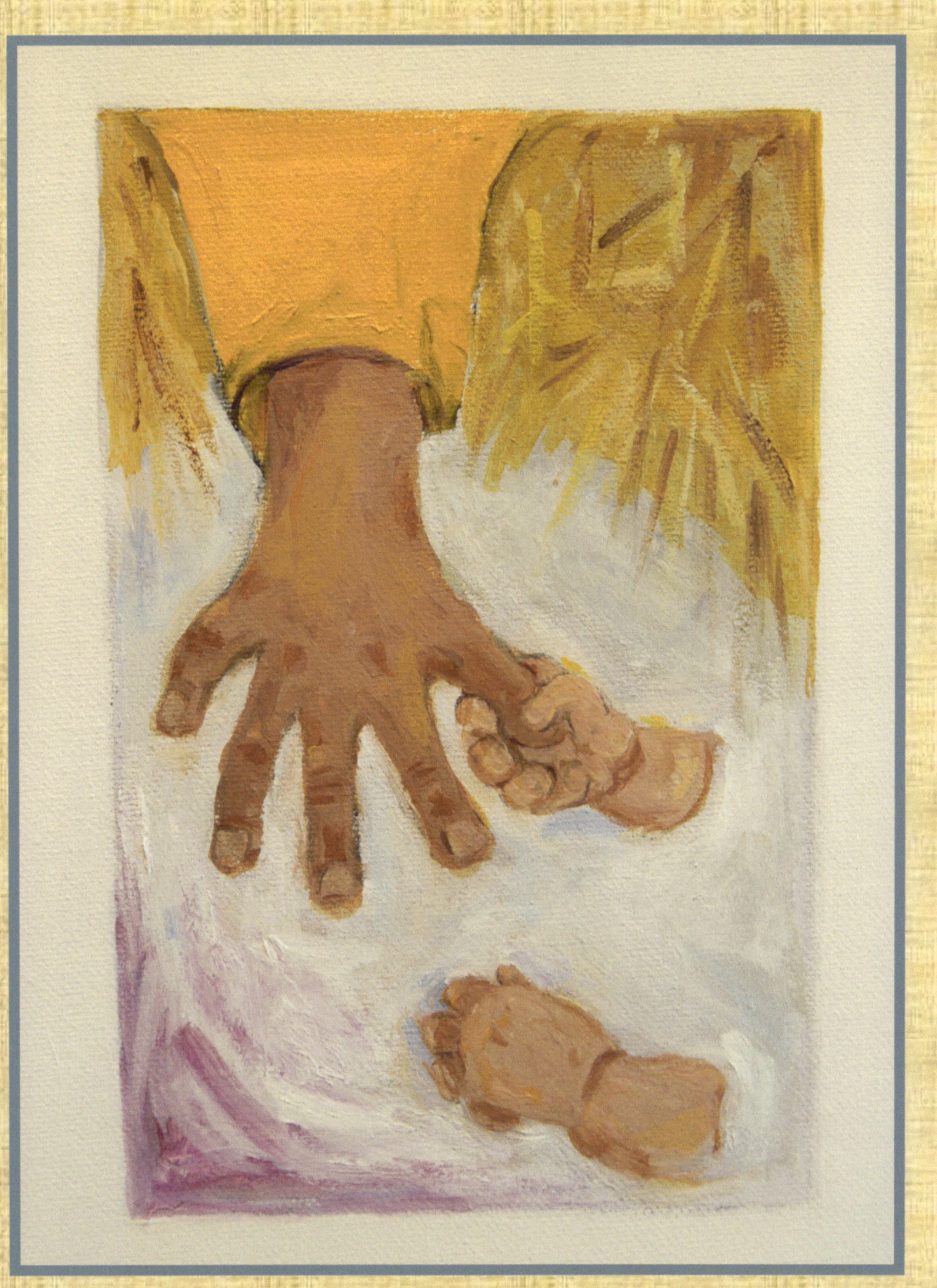

About the Illustrator

Gloria P. Weisz has taught elementary school and college art. She can often be found at her easel or working with clay in her Atlanta, Georgia, studio.

About the Author

Dwyn Mounger is a pastor who often, by Christmas Eve candlelight, tells the story of Elihu to children gathered around him. He is a grandfather of four.

For information regarding permission, write to the publisher or author:
Crippled Beagle Publishing
5413 Glen Cove Drive, Knoxville, Tennessee 37919
dyer.cbpublishing@gmail.com
(865) 414-4017

Dwyn Mounger
(865) 249-7731 ~ (904) 315-9312)
dwynmounger@gmail.com

www.ingramcontent.com/pod-product-compliance
Lightning Source LLC
Chambersburg PA
CBHW041124070526
44584CB00003B/276